also by Sasha Dugdale

POETRY

Notebook
The Estate
Red House
Joy
Deformations

TRANSLATION

Birdsong on the Seabed
[ELENA SHVARTS]

The Grainstore
Bad Roads
[NATALYA VOROZHBIT]

In Memory of Memory
War of the Beasts and the Animals
Holy Winter 20 / 21
[MARIA STEPANOVA]

SASHA DUGDALE

The Strongbox

CARCANET

First published in Great Britain in 2024 by Carcanet,
Alliance House, 30 Cross Street, Manchester, M2 7AQ
www.carcanet.co.uk

A CIP catalogue record for this book is available from the British Library.

ISBN: 978-1-800-17-408-5

Designed & Typeset for Sasha Dugdale by John Morgan.

The publisher acknowledges financial assistance
from Arts Council England.

The Strongbox

I can only count the lice I have popped
with a candle, said Homer.
The rest are stuck in the seams.

I. ANATOMY OF AN ABDUCTION

Morning light, crazed like a delft tile.

Three blue figures bent over a frame
coffee on the stove
and repairing
> *snip*

repairing
> *snip*

Heavy shears clatter on the table.

Evenings on the sofa
three old women
in the shapeshifting beam of the telly
poking strands of cloth through a net
to make familiar the stone cold hearth,
rags made from dresses and towels
from sheets and aprons
rags stripped and ripped
from shoulders and hips
far too soon

> *electric bars*
> *and a relief of heaped plastic coals*
> *through which flames rise*
> *always in the same measure*
> *kindled and consuming*
> *then waning*

so other fires can spring up
always in the same measure

This is where the small children lay
absorbed by the light's trick
watching the shadows play
the ticking of the electric.

Upstairs landscape of the bedroom,
secret landscape for one:
tiny with a pine shelf of fluffy toys
posters, nail gels, glitter pens
a perspex presentation box for the pink halves
of her birth egg.

Outside the Taygetus, like a dark arcade of shops
old and silent at night
when, after duties, after religious classes
the midnight chats
    back and forth
once her friends
    but now just him.

It began with the sun
appearing over the plane wing
supernatural orange
                          but no light

A night of bitter memories
sitting bolt upright
phrase book on her lap
travelling east

fire, yes, the opposite of sea
but sea is light, too
cracking open a bright ravine
through the waves
for the rising sun
to pass through

It began on the least good road
late at night, a silent soldier
sent to bring her here
his leather pouch on the passenger seat
his bow slung over his shoulder

The road signs deteriorate
                              ever smaller
    bent and battered
    busted
    bullet-holed
The roads incline.

They stopped at roadside inns twice,
and twice she waited in the cold and silence
the music abated
the mountain stars above

She's told not to open the door
so she huddles, draws her furred hood tighter
the chill of leatherette under her thighs
smell of petrol from jerrycans

she need only light a match
and the whole lot *whump*

just the blackened skeleton of the pickup
men scattering from the inn door

Not too late to run
                    but where to?
hadn't the fates conspired
to weave her bridal shroud
watching her
with their one eye hanging
    from the rear-view.

Too late too late
too much has passed

Love came and ripped out her heart
replaced it with a burning coal

folding air tickets into a travel pouch
and promises of gifts
swatches of wedding silk
a garnet brooch
to bleed out in her spongebag

and here she is dabbing wax on her lips
on the cold slippery back seat
in a high altitude layby.

  all requites fire and fire requites all
  so coins are needed to purchase fine cloth
  and cloth given in return for gold
  but a woman entwisted in fine cloth
  may herself be purchased, or stolen

We are so close to the ground in childhood
we weave the tiny sappy strings of daisies
gather the broken china of an egg

The worm convulses gently on my palm
lying under the lavender

So bees shake pollen on your cheek
and apples, apples, as many as we can eat
rolling on the lawn
    but when I reached out a hand
    he saw me
and all was lost.

A huddled pair at the station
at the brazier with their cardboard cases
old woman and a bundled child
(the stranger from the south who promised them a bed)
and no one ever saw them again

The woman's shoes kick at the bottom of a canal
the buckles reflecting moonlight
through oily shadows.

That could have been you! dark child
blond child in a felt blanket
resting in a manger
    make haste innocents
    trust no one
your train pulling in on a ghostly platform
last train of the last night
    run!

Or the lure,
a piece of red meat
a chop on a hook
lowered over a wall,
or the snatch
flagrant
from the back of a car
at a shopping mall.

The search party, the single sighting,
the handmade posters. 'We love her
we know she's out there
we just want her back.'

Or yelling yelling
in the dark woods at dusk
listening for sounds so intently

(the scrabble on leaves
a sudden patter,
accumulated rain sliding from a branch
to the ground)

that the thud of your own heart
startles you into flight.

She passes long hours rehearsing her bridal vow
with a pillow under her
in place of a man who was just
   wow!
   all muscles all supple-skinned
   heaven-sent
   angel-face

who threw her an apple
who made her promise—

But does it matter what she promised
or what she turned her back on
to be in his warrior embrace?

Yes, I too have studied the science of parting
there was a press conference, I sat veiled
was asked whether I had given up my rights
that night when with hair loosed
I bent down to examine the wax—

or when I opened my door
and tiptoed by the wan glow of the nightlight
left over from when small children
strayed on the landing
and their mother scooped them up to soothe them—

I slid across the bolt that barred the door
holding to my chest a sports bag
and there outside an unlit car in meagre light
heralded the new.

Did she say goodbye, did she wave
did she genuflect, text—

did she blow a kiss
as she slunk down the stairs
or think of her brothers
still asleep in their bunk
baby fists
resting on superhero sheets

did she offer prayers of thanks
did she pass between childhood
and marriage
like a hostage
thrown from one phalanx
onto the sand
in front of the other—

this fire that finds its natural measure
like a lock gate through which
tiny spurts and streams fall
on the rising black water

soon it will be level
on either side
and the heavy gate
swings unhindered

fire not the opposite of water
but its reflection
burns in the great year
and on in the next
so the door between years
swings unhindered

It was favourite uncle who beat her
with cable with a chair leg with a belt
while the others looked on
and if her husband had gone by then
    she no longer loved him
For he must have had other girls
prisoners, slaves, other wives

And she too
slept nightly
with another.

Everything is woven
the pillows stuffed with feathers
after they killed and plucked the bird
that strutted in the courtyard,
in the filthy hut
had her name
                    scratched out
meaning   *shining light*
meaning   *fragrant*

Was she born from an egg
    a reptile, the daughter of a whore
    a dragon biting the hand that raised her
was she drawn into a barbaric cult
    a murderous city kingdom
was it plainly speaking her fault?

Did she ask for pardon
did she express remorse
wouldn't any man on any ship
if he'd dared to set his sights so?
Would he not have taken her
himself? Even now with the pillow
on her lap, legs wide, in slippers,
bawling her eyes out, kohl
marking her cheeks.
Even now—

For men the bronze, for women
wax, although she never divined her fate
merely followed it, like pulling on string
tore itself stickily away

The old women in the kitchen
with their long shears, their bubbling pots
punish the young
                                    and are punished in turn
slaps on the nape of the neck

They are pure, at least they talk a good deal
about purity   in this city
where war is the father of all
They slip off shoes at the doors
and always after wrestling or shooting
slaves run strigils over their naked backs
and before they are dressed in laundered gowns
they are rubbed with oils and unguents
forbidden to use deodorants or products
or pain relief   or even gas at the dentist
strapping weapons on themselves, brandishing pikes
standing three to a chariot
they are like the heroes in children's tales
sleeping on dry bracken after a swim.

You know how it says
no one steps in the same river twice
    always scattering in the grasp
She has a dream in the wretched cellar
so very far from home
although when she wakes nothing is real

only slowly becomes real
as she wakes and the dream, lapping
recedes

But in the dream she knew she'd had this dream before
within the dream the dream announced itself
as a repeating dream
within her dream there is a past
contained in recognition, that aching sense
that moves just ahead of her
                              like water
that she has been here before
that she's been here eternally before

The dream was of a freezing desert
(hard to capture a dream because it moves just ahead
it seems there, but it isn't, always partly clothed)
but the sky was speckled with stars
and this journey through the vast cold nothing
led to something beyond her wildest
(but she was perhaps confused, was this not space?
did there exist such a wild place on the globe?)
Every wild place is simply the edge of our wildest
but to another it is the centre

She would not be surprised to see
a group of women eating
under a frozen tree on a plain,
arboreous chandelier
raining its glass on them where they pass food about
lipstick on their mouths in the wilderness
skirts and scarves
and the tree scattering its crystal shock

It could just be a spasm of memory
or it could be a picnic
under a frozen plum tree
in outer space

Morning again
although the sun is no more than a human foot
treading its way across the yard
to bring news
but first the call and response

    glory to the city and its heroes!
        glory to its heroes!

then

    the sun goes dim in old age!
        and is lit again in youth!

and finally the password

    filth cleanses   chill heats   river parches
        but the sun is reborn with the day

the shutters thrown back
the light admitted.

One of them, a boy, despite the beard
makes birds out of foil wrapping
when no one's looking
and finger silhouettes of wolves
tongues flapping on the wall

He crouches with his arms on his knees
and blows smoke rings
   he's bored, taken his eye off the prize
   he won't last long
but I can't help smiling can't help
sliding my hand through the bars
to cradle the golden bird
   is that wrong?

They are men with a losing hand
on a losing streak
backed the wrong horse
on their uppers
climbing the shabby staircase
to look out over a vast arid plain
where they staked their hopes
and left them to perish.

Hope?
     a straw-filled figure
repeatedly run through with spears
wielded by auxiliaries on a training ground

waves of young dancers walking at the target
bearing high shields
            and chanting

   ADVANCE   CLOSE IN   KILL

And closer in, the figure
              leaks
its tied limbs made of wounds
its belly a gaping hole
in the calico

13

outmatch it in aggression
or you got a fight on your hands
simple as

It is true, I said
that morning in the basement
we thought we had nothing left
but day after day we were losing,
one after another brought home
defiled, dust-stained
all their life's moisture
smeared across the punishing grit,
haemorrhaging loss, it seemed
we could lose no more:
every new handful scooped from a vast heap of loss
and yet when we sang, we sang the gods' praises
we sang of riches we had once enjoyed.

Truly I dreamt of nothing but home
although like all nostalgia it was false
the golden light of evening then the gloam
and everything gentle   unforced
shadowed laughing features   a conversation out of reach
a cine film   my brothers tumbling from their saddles
scent of sunscreen   the gnarled root in a peach
a lizard basking   a paper boat twisting in the eddies
the moment a milk tooth unfastens from the gum
or how it felt when once I sucked my thumb.

But I can't be sure of ever having owned such an array
of recollected moments

Did the memory begin with me or was it always
chugging idly like an engine
jolting like a hen without a head

egg   chicken   egg   chicken   egg

and is remembering merely the sudden exposure
of dream? As when the border guard drags film
from the camera's body—is recall
the fatal undoing of the sealed?

I cried out sharply   the film hung spoiled.

And if this happened at all, did it happen again
folding into one
as the bellows needed for sound and flame
collapse in a wavering drone?

Even as I rang the number on the slip
I saw little chance of escape
I left a message in the pre-arranged code
ripped the paper to bits

Disguise? It was beyond me
I radiated   just as saints will
when they appear as an iridescent filmy tower
their glittery souls overflowing
in sheaves like sparkling water
on grain silos   or above the site of a chemical spill
on the eves and anniversaries of disaster
to warn   to grieve

and just as governments send helicopters
with searchlights
bowls of neon upended

light sprays its power shower
to dim
and drown the immortal blaze

and troops are dispatched
to erect barriers on all major routes
turn back   repel   arrest
all pilgrims who are drawn
to see
and be blest

yes I could have worn bandages
over a face covered in sores
a scaly body
a tragedy mask

my godhead would still have been manifest
my grace
unsurpassed

A city like a golden crown on a grassy head
a golden crown athwart the head of a prince
and little galloping flags
scatter over the plain

In the foreground a boy leads an ass

The ass lowers its powerful neck to pull at grass
and the boy lifts his stick to drive it on

for all beasts are driven with blows
and the ass can't distinguish between home
and wayside grass.

Closer up, this city shudders with a muted music
a thin stream of car horns, traffic, mingling voices
(all its discord all its variance)
china clinking in tea houses
calves drawn in a line to slaughter
the rasping knife in the cabbage's core
the pallets stacked in the market place
parakeets on the swinging wires
barrel organs, smoke, smoke alarms
plazas of stone used for dances
and now for shooting practice.
All this variance brought like strands of sound
into attunement, a murmuring
like the harmony of bees
over a child's flushed face
as she lies under the lavender

   so the thrust and the parry
   draw combatants into loving proximity
   into an embrace, bodies distanced only
   by the limit of an axe
   so music too pits note against note
   lunging line against checking arm
   to make harmony, to entwine
   bodies in mortal harm

The morning twinkles on cafe tables
wet with dew, but the plate glass windows
are smashed and boarded up
so the lyres are stopped

locked away. Nests are flown
their eggs grown cold.

The bored guy in the yard sits nearer to my window
like a dog shifting daily closer
laying itself, slumping down
as if merely following the sun
never looking my way

He's sanding arrow shafts
ready for their bronze nibs
his bow placed out in the dust
his most treasured possession
directly in line with my window

all I'd have to do is reach out and tickle his ear
he's longing to tell me

tongue-tied   but longing
he's longing   to tell me
never looking   tongue-tied
longing to loose   his tongue
I reach out   to tousle his hair
to set his tongue   loose

His bow is of wood with a handle of bone
'Its arc,' he says, 'is the arc of life
curving up to the midpoint in its prime:
the sun at noon, the prow of the archer's chest,
stretching to dispatch its slender missile.
How it descends fast—as fast as the sun!
racing down towards the far sea
to plunge itself into non-existence.

'Or, as the poet begins his purple song
with long languid lines, singing of arms
so enamoured of his lovely voice,
he climbs slowly to the apex
gripping the mike, whispering:

> *the mortal hero dealt a sudden blow*
> *and bleeding out his mortal juices*
> *takes up arms against the foe*
> *brings spear to shoulder and releases—*

Now your poet's ablaze like Zeus!
whipping up the words in a lather
of horror, of disaster!

> *Flinching as he courses*
> *through the dust.*
> *One final thrust and all is lost*
> *for the tamer of horses…'*

He brings his dirty finger down the bow's polished wood
to where he's wedged it in a patch of thyme.
'You're funny,' I say. 'You rhyme.'

He grins (toothless)
'They laugh at archers but we're ruthless.
They say we're crooked, but I once shot a man in the foot
and he never walked straight again.'

II. IN THE REHEARSAL ROOM

Ok, people, good to see you all back so promptly. Thanks for that. I like to start on time.

Right. Can we make a little ring with our chairs?

(*Pause. Sound of chairs scraping*)

Nice one. We're going to do an exercise now. We've had a readthrough and I think we're all there with the text, etc. So what I'd like to do is this. You've all heard of *actioning*?

(*Pause*)

Thought so. Good, good. Standard stuff, but it can yield some insights, I find. Especially at the beginning of the rehearsal process, and it can be invaluable with a tricky text or one that doesn't initially appear to have a narrative.

So, I'd like to get us into groups of two—or three. I think we have someone over if we go into groups of two, no? Yes. Ok. You can be a threesome, so to speak. Now I'd like you each to take a fragment and just *action* it line by line. I know this can be unfamiliar so let's just do a group one together so we all have the hang of it.

For example in the speech 'It is true, I said'. Yep? Found that one? Page fourteen on your script.

Lovely, lovely. So here we go:

> It is true, I said, that morning in the basement,
> we thought we had nothing left, but... day after
> day we were losing, one after another... brought
> home... defiled... dust-stained...

What do we think are the *actions* that underpin that text there?

If you want to think of it more loosely as, you know, a *gestus* in the Brechtian sense, that can be useful.

I think it may help if we stick to verbs as well. Which verbs are the machines behind this little piece? What is actually going on? What's the author trying to make happen here?

Yep. Right. We've got a... Can you say that again?

'Anguish'. Ok. Anguish... Anguish is really more of an abstract state, right? Can we transform it into a verb? A doing word? A word of *action*.

...In fact, people, can we steer clear of abstraction here. Let's stick to verbs. I want the concrete. The truth is concrete as Bert Brecht says—

Yep, no, 'hopelessness' won't do either.

I want *active agency*. Important to remember *active agency* in battle at all times. Otherwise, where's the conflict, the dynamic? If we can't identify it, what do we present as we speak the lines?

If you like, where's the fight if you can't lift the sword?
There are times when stasis doesn't cut the mustard.

After all I like to see
the blossoming tree, but only my
disgust at the speeches of the warmonger
brings me to the rehearsal room.

III. THE BREAKERS' YARD

With the viewing binoculars rotated
the metal barrels angled to her face
the eyepieces pressed at her skin with a cold flashbulb ache.

She dropped in a coin
                and now

she could divide them into warships
and merchant navy.

    Of the warships:
bulbous destroyers, spindly frigates in airfix grey,
some tattered ships of the line
tugged by steamers to their last resting place.

    Of the merchant navy:
listing steamships,
a few ocean liners spewing black smoke,
clown-shoe tankers, freight vessels sent for scrap.

    Small boats included:
navy vessels such as the fast patrollers,
auxiliaries, landing craft, also pilot boats and tugs,
flat-bottomed coal boats tossed unnaturally by the waves,
yachts and dinghies, rowing boats, galleys,
boats made of leaf and reed and hide.

They made their fictional appearance every day—
every day a wedge of snowgeese rising above the plain.

Each had a history:
in one a surgeon had operated knee-deep in water,
another was the president's wife's yacht,
a third the unlucky *Struma*.

It was clear only she could see them.
They were equal in number to her nightmares.
She too contained bulwarks and powder kegs.
She bruised easily. Her gums often bled.

They waited but never docked or moored
or sent out signals. It was as if they were
waiting to pass through straits.

She stood motionless on the concrete pedestal.
Her dress falling to her feet
in a thousand stiff folds.

They were her opposites. They were sent
to define her. She in turn to wreck them.

How must it feel to be Cassandra—
endlessly touting your translations of dire words
to soldiers, kings, chieftains, their queens
and to hear, over and over again:
sorry, not this time . . . not quite our thing . . .
thank you for thinking of us.

You know, says Cassandra, that your voice is ugly.
Between pitches you sit
bemused in an office chair
holding a cup and a teabag.

It is not your civilisation
they want to hear from—
It's the future that's a foreign country.

Once, says Cassandra, I brought my words to a warrior.
What is this? he shouted at me.
It's irony, I whispered, but very quietly.
I prophesied I would die on the spot—
but got that one wrong.

Even you couldn't bear it.

The stories were too real. There was no craft—
all of it could easily have come about.

No room was left for the imagination.
It wasn't so much art as social project.

Whenever you saw her you felt guilty.

Often I am dispatched on a liner
towering over the city.
It makes hospitable the inhospitable sea
by displacing a great volume of danger.
Large as an upside-down pyramid
and calm as a tranquiliser, it contains
multitudes of potted palms, chairs
and tapestries of nereids
its black engine revolves and quakes
in a white chasm under an iron grid.
I call it Andromache and sit
where I cannot hear it bellyache.

Once Captain saw a glint in the waves
and turned the ship—
this was no ordinary nautical feat
it took a hundred days.
In pursuit of that tiny flash we got lost
saw sea monsters in the fog
the engine twitched like a dreaming dog
the ship now way off course—
It was an unopened can of sprats
but by then we were in untracked seas
beyond the Pillars of Herakles
off the maps.

pigs bathe in the miry puddle
washing every scrap from their girth
with new quantities of sticky earth
bathed, yet freshly muddy

chickens groom and strut
in the yard's bathhouse,
raising great dustclouds
to wash out the smut

MENELAUS: Seven gods made seven men, gave them seven women. Each pair had seven children. Each pair had seven goats.

HELEN: Seven pots? Seven pairs of pants?

MENELAUS: Each of these seven had seven children more. And then they too had seven.

HELEN: Where are we now?

MENELAUS: Look, I'll draw it for you:

G   G   G   G   G   G   G

These are Capital G Gods

```
M      M      M      M      M      M      M
W      W      W      W      W      W      W
/ \    / \    / \    / \    / \    / \    / \
```

Ok, now I have to write really small.

BBBBGGG   BBBGGGG   BBBBGGG   BBBGGGG   BBBBGGG   BBBGGGG   BBBBGGG

I've done it so they have alternating numbers of boys and girls. Some have four boys and some have four girls. Of course you can't predict how many boys or girls a couple will have although men may inherit a genetic tendency to have one or the other. However over time the population remains approximately balanced, so for a myth I think this layout is pretty good.

So, this generation, the boys and girls, they all have to get together with the children from other families because they're basically the only ones around. Now it gets a bit complicated. I'm going to draw in this patch of sand:

MW MW MW MW MW MW MW MW MW MW MW MW MW MW MW MW MW MW MW MW MW MW MW MW

See, there are 24 pairs and each of these has seven children

$$24 \times 7 = 168$$

I need to move to the ground over here to have the space for all these.

HELEN: Wait a minute. I'm still counting...

MENELAUS: ...Alright.

HELEN: There's one spare. You left one out.

MENELAUS: I'm sorry?

HELEN: Maybe a boy, maybe a girl, but someone's been left out. 7 lots of 7 is 49, an odd number, not 24 pairs.

MENELAUS: What? Oh. Alright. I'll put another person here. M or W? Doesn't matter which.

His wife shrugs

MENELAUS: Fine, I'll just do a dot. Anyway back to the 168. Happily that *is* an even number, so 84 couples each producing another seven children, which I make 588. Another even number.

HELEN: But what happens to the dot person? Are they, like, a spare? a swap? for when the maths goes wrong? Or a lone electron strolling the rows of marital bonds?

MENELAUS: I don't think this is—

HELEN: I mean, just having a loner out there... a 'dot'... it destabilises things...

MENELAUS: Ah yes, well, if I can explain—

HELEN: ...someone to peer from the bushes into the campfire circle...

MENELAUS: ...because I think you aren't getting the point of this...

HELEN: ...someone to look in everyone's window at night...

MENELAUS: Or maybe you're being deliberately difficult. But if I can finish?

She shrugs again

MENELAUS: It's a myth, a beautiful shape. It's how they

thought of the beginning. Seven Gods. Seven couples. Seven intermixed tribes.

And you mentioned destabilisation earlier. Let me come back to that point.

The glory of seven, you see, is that in any conflict situation there will always be inequality. A strength on one side—or the other. There will never be an exactly-matched battle. Either you have three tribes against four, or two against five, and so on. So conflict doesn't just drag on unnecessarily. Whatever the argument, whatever the cause, there will always be a clear winner.

Conflict is Justice. You see my point? It's a beautiful structure, if you ignore that one small mistake in my counting.

HELEN: It wasn't a mistake, it's just there's a person spare and your myth doesn't account for them. Where do they go? What do they do? Are they the cause of all that conflict you've built into your beautiful shape?

If there's a shape and it contains its own conflict, better to acknowledge that, surely?

MENELAUS: It's frustrating talking to you. It's like you see a beautiful piece of cloth and you always have to tug on a loose thread. You see a pattern and you point out where it doesn't match. You always have to disagree.

Why can't you see things as I present them to you? Why the constant discord?

HELEN: But you were the one talking about discord. I mean all this is about war, isn't it—

MENELAUS: Why the contempt for me and all I stand for?

And when I think I took you back—no need at all to bring you home. I could have left you to your death, dispatched you with my own bare hands. After all, you said it first—you've done immeasurable harm.

V. MEN & GODS

At high tide the river swelled its banks.
Thin sedge grasses glittered in the water
and wading birds lifted from the shallows—

Here comes Tricky-eel-rests-in-sand and
Eel-back-glints-in-mud, with spears both
and plans to appease the river god

here further up stands Flashing-trout-belly
and Unsmiling-carp-bursts-up-glop!
all without their armour, just their wellies

nets and lines in hand they wait,
in each man's head what to take
and what to leave

for the river god is quick to wrath
and if you take too much on credit
he'll rise from his sodden hearth

and place you in bond to war—
your children too, and all your kin
he'll gore you and retrieve his loss

he'll flick with his powerful fin
the swallowed fish back up your throat
he'll lay you to dry on a bank

he'll flay your sunburned flank
and leave you afloat
a dish for the eagle and the crow—

or you meander, a naked ghost,
and another marks in you the albatross
and lets loose an arrow.

  water at once polluted and pure
  blue as cobalt, as lapis, as the sky
  but the fish breathe heavy on the banks
  and an army drank there, sickened and died

Is it lawful, asks Apollo, for me
to cut the honey-sweet grass of her bed?

Kheiron considers this
his face gentle, impassive
(because much is at stake)
but his tail swishes impatiently
and he shifts from hoof to hoof as he replies:

Imagine we were inhabitants of a new planet
fertile but without history
rivers   lush grassland
mountains   seas

You can't tread time like water—
everything you do is recorded
when there are no records,
like a baby's first steps.

Some roll boulders from distant hills
        then dress the stone
some roam the plains on ponies
        to find pastureland
while others wail, burn aromatic oils
        and daub dreams on cave walls.

No speech yet, but one day fiercely polished metal
will reveal the gods are not picked out in stars.

But you, Lord, you know the history.
You know how it begins and ends.
You've sung it so many times.

There is one race of men, another of gods.
As one whose lovely feet roam
both camps, I once dreamt I was caught
uninvited, in the divine beachside home

I had poured the gods' olive oil,
drunk from their cups, picked flowers they'd planted,
worse still I had no memory.
Had I asked permission? Had it been granted?

I'll tidy here   I'll clear the rubble   I'll smarten the altar
take the first boat out and no one will know
I'll disappear over the water
I'll swim if needs be   I'll steal oars and row

But these thoughts, in the manner of nightmares,
accompanied the approaching shrieks

of gods wearing lurex, feathers and furs
with hooked claws and marble cheeks

Knowing I'd been caught *in flagrante*
I repented of such unforgivable sinning
and offered my necklace of polished antler
Zeus plucked it from me, all the while grinning

then passed it to Hera. Her hair was ochre
and I had crossed her, I was ensnared,
they drew me into their fierce circle
to rip at me, cuff me, drag me upstairs

I knew what would come
and perhaps that was the dream
that their race will forever screw over the other
but destroys all those who stand in-between.

VI. THE DIRTY FIRE

You are not yet gone.
They told me where you were and when you left,
I could still catch you if I hurried
not stand around wasting my breath.

I caught you up, but you'd died down—
in your place a brown patch.
I knew I'd have to pour petrol
over your tender features and strike a match.

In the dirty fire of the great poets
there are lines of such naturalness
that when you have torched the source
you too must end in wordlessness.

At odds with everything in the fall
of my life, I fell to my knees.
I was a heretic, but no longer—
I'm heartened by your simplicities.

Let me exist underground with the iris
slowly opening my pale hands.
My workings are unbearable.
My renewal what the world demands.

Out of water comes soul
and as it lifts—

39

Slippery-eel-on-my-spear
is ready for it

He's been training for this moment for months
since he was given his tourniquets
his buckets of salt

Soul swells with red
but eludes the point
and Slippery drops his weapon
and grabs his foot
                    Ai!

Come-home-empty-handed would be a better name
for a boy with so little promise

He climbs the steep road to the city
pails clanking in his hands
where morning is now in full swing
the trams passing each other
He shows a fig to the cast iron statue
stepping down from its chariot
to slay the dawn's only child
with a spear

fired in a ball of heat
and then colonised
by peaceable pigeons

   such marvellous deaths
   are assigned destinies of more magnitude

Sometimes he has a cone on his head.

Graces, muses, Frau Minne

I had to die back, I dried out, left
a silhouette
a teasel, a brown umbel

gave up a mouth, an eye that drew beauty
but the features hung together a while
after the face withered

and still longer the pain quelled up
before returning to its dark owner

and when I next poked my head above the earth
everything I remembered was gone
only wasteland strip lighting
and women stepping over rubble

                                 It was morning
mist lay over the plain and campfires burned
two armies two machines squared up for the new day

kings debated whether I would be caught
in caterpillar treads or chariot wheels

so low to the ground
I had the perfect view

It was terrible I suppose
but although I ached a little
with the cramped quarters
and my sight had deteriorated
it was still better to be alive

all around the seas had gathered to watch
currents rerouted rivers rewired
for one must run to put out violence
it spreads faster than fire

Down there I rolled my thoughts in the darkness
spreading my dirt-clotted filaments

I dived down to inspect my strongboxes
got used to it, the dereliction, the dim bulb

Carried out my rituals at the year's end
discovered I was not what I thought I was
knew not what I had become

the miracle of the tuber
to fan itself through dense earth with such deliberate
refinement
each translucent thread parting matter and time

this time of the cycle you can split a root bundle
although every thought will snag and squeal,
and if properly divided, properly rendered,
will make a new identity

As usual I looked through everything
all the oval objects, the ancestral eggs
polished them, reworded their messages

where one had read:

if only you knew
what rubbish gave root to poetry

I made it:

the muck from which a poem sprouts
if you could only see

then:

how I flourished
on the manure heap

what a shame
in a midden
in a trench
on a plain

only yesterday
she ran wringing her hands

but now she's off having intrigues
and her laugh, so pleasing, so low,
and what has been and what will be
she doesn't care to know

Demeter
came to me in a dream
asking why I'd paid no mind to her tale;
I died thereafter
and appeared myself
to an old woman
saying here's one you can have for free:

Sultry desolate beach
accessible even in war

via a track that once serviced oil wells
running behind the dunes
car tyre treads between two threads of barbed wire
it isn't Lake Geneva, that's for sure

On the one hand a sewage breach
on the other
faint popping of shells
distant tunes

   a dead skate
   tail dead straight
   like a goose in reverse

o the jelly-twigs of thought

it's been safe here for weeks
under the pitched roof of a magazine
a bronze mother breathes deep,
                  her child
a girl in the fertile crescent of life
playing nearby

SCANDAL OF HER SECRET ELOPEMENT
THE ANTI-HERO ROLE THAT MADE HIM A LEGEND

A TRAGIC END IN THE SPRINGTIME OF HER LIFE
TROUBLED STAR ACTS MACHO TO PROVE HIS FATHER
  WRONG

THE DOWNFALL OF A DIVA
ARREST FOR A CRIME OF PASSION
I HAD EATING DISORDER CONFESSES UNHAPPY BRIDE

except I don't like such conjunctures:
flattery is a warm bath
but celebrity is a creature
of the earth

a ship
was sunk
in harbour
today

no bombshell
from the dustbowl
has the security
of bronze

heavens
an abode
a safe locker
for the immortal

Coral telephone
foaming listener
can you put me through
to my sister?

resist this sea-motion
it has you in its grip!
she is begging you
to board the last ship

from here on in is death
you who faints at blood!
here is devastation
turn back
turn back
my love

I have been led
to a marsh
by a hairless child
and my soul is moist

my glasses are salty
I am full of fluster
I send you a wave
my semblable—my sister

August is a hopeless month
lost wasps jostle on the mottled fruit

In August cooks do battle with bluebottles
armed with flypapers of arsenic green

Damn this heat!
slops simmer in the mess—

In August tyrants send their men to the villas
where bare-chested rivals are sipping anis

In August the itinerant army
has been on the road too long
and the ground is too hard

the crew hammer home
splayed and blunted pegs
and dark arguments brew

sickly apricots dangling
so many you can't stop
so fragrant
          the stink

queues at the makeshift latrines
bowels distended, men bowed over

a man slits his own throat
with a slither of glass
his body plonked among prickly reeds

in late August he appears in a dream
and says:

Souls can smell in Hades
and I can smell your unsheathed soul
Want to know how you smell?
like kidneys fried in butter.

Oh the injustice!
We flit behind you
on the banks of the Lethe
salivating in our ghostly gobs
Any one of us unburied millions
would devour you in a second.

VII. FIRST & SECOND DREAMS

HELEN comes to in a sweat, puts out a hand.

HELEN. Are you awake? I had a bad dream.

PARIS (*drowsy, takes her hand in his*). It's ok now. You're here with me.

HELEN. Can I tell you? It had such... clarity.

PARIS. Sure...

HELEN. I was walking the dog down to the park. An evening walk, the last of the day and it was already dusk, the light was failing.

PARIS begins snoring lightly.

HELEN. And I went into the castle park, the one with the grassy mound where the ramparts once were. And as I walked alongside the mound I heard *them*...

PARIS is suddenly awake and listening.

They were on the top of the mound. They had a camp-fire. I could see the light from it and hear it crackling. They were singing around the fire. I could understand them, of course.

PARIS. What were they singing?

HELEN. It was very clear and distinct. They were singing: *European buyers for Greek poppy.* And even though I'm not speaking their language now, I knew that refrain.

PARIS. And then?

HELEN. I slipped away and came back. I was trembling... afraid to be caught.

PARIS springs out of bed and begins dressing. He straps his weapons to his belt.

HELEN. What are you doing?

PARIS. They'll have tracked you here... I'll go and sleep in the apartment across the landing tonight.

*

HELEN wakes with a muffled cry. The fan is a steady hum overhead.

PARIS. What is it, my pet? Another dream?

HELEN. Yes.

PARIS. Tell me.

HELEN (*pauses*). There's a funny thing with dreams. As you tell them they come into being. Until you say them aloud, the story of them... it's there and not there.

PARIS. Hmm.

HELEN. As you recount them they start to exist.

PARIS is losing interest.

HELEN. What is a dream and what is it not? (*pause*) I was in their vaulted and lofty war council.

PARIS is now alert, like a dog that has heard something in the yard.

HELEN. It wasn't so much a tent as an academic classical theatre. Maybe a conservatoire. Thousands of people sitting in red velvet chairs. And the light was vast. There were columns holding up the roof—

(but he doesn't want to hear about the architecture)

A group of their commanders was on the stage, sitting in a semi-circle, talking to the people below.

PARIS. What were they saying?

HELEN. I don't know, I couldn't—

PARIS. Think!

HELEN. I was in bed... Lying in a metal-framed hospital bed, and the bed was up there on the stage. But it was positioned behind them, and so to begin with it was as if they couldn't see me and I couldn't hear them. They were all there, the swift and the hyacinthine, talking to the immense audience. The most violent man alive was sitting forward in his chair and his boots shone. It was he who first seemed to notice me. Or perhaps he noticed that I was awake and watching. He came around to the bedside. He leaned over me—

HELEN pauses.

PARIS. Go on.

HELEN. The next bit... I can hardly bear to say it... because saying it brings it into being.

PARIS. What did he do?

HELEN. All I can say, is that it... you must believe me... it wasn't an erotic dream.

PARIS springs out of bed in a fury.

VIII. AN EMPTY STAGE

Death came to the plain and perched in a tree

She wore a riding habit with puffed sleeves
Her shoulder blades were a pattern of kohl-ringed eyes
Tweed skirt falling in stiff folds behind her

When she turned her head it was stumpy
Foreshortened

Wherever she directed her gaze there was absence

Doors softly closed
Doves tucked into their cots
Deer froze

The day held its breath
The sun stopped to watch

The beeches are there to calm us
their roots are polished by weather,
four sets of protruding knuckles
or clavicles
or smooth knees—
as if the end of life had come upon them
on a blustery day
and they had simply lifted their hands
and knelt down on the bank.

Then Philemon shook his head in silent wonder
and beech mast swarmed like bees
and when Baucis opened her mouth to speak
she roared like a machine in a mill—

The truth is
              Philemon was trailing behind
dragging a shopping trolley through the mud
when Baucis trod on a mine

She begged him for water and he had none.
He stroked her head, her lips ·
There was nothing to be done
and so he
              he spoke to her
all the while
              in that darkness
he never once ran out of words

How untidy the word is
trailing ribbons and studded with eyes
    wet white flesh
when the spade cuts deep

toss the words into a heap
    clumped in mud
    flat-earth-tabula
raised from darkness
    out of joint
    guttering
or glittering with mildew
    like an old cloak

twelve of them
    a prophetic number

the death of darkness
is the birth of air

thirty! the Rubicon!
    bearers of the law of
    subterranean constellations.

sweet order when the freckled words
    their knotted strings
are heaped on the surface

big   small
    scarred by the prong
blighted   thrush song

On the street outside, a car's passing headlamp.
Still day and it diffuses into sunlight but
A brightness infects the air:
·A small pail of phosphorus
Swept across the asphalt with a quick broom
And when it's gone the day seems darker

As when towards twilight a vapour trail
Opens its neon zip in the sky

Could be dawn could be dusk
The only difference being that
Dawn has no memory whereas dusk
Remembers everything—

Reluctant traveller, it pauses,
Attempts to look over its shoulder
As the night chases it across the sky
Catching the straggling clouds
Beating them blue and purple and green.

Still, dusk hangs at the edge of all
As night comes on with fists flashing.
Remember me, remember me, it calls
As it fades and grows cold, remember this—
This is the last time you will see me.

All night the record crackles on the turntable
Until dawn trips in and lifts the stylus
Riddles the ash and sets the fire
Checks the mirror, fingers her face, thinking
Who the hell am I?

Is it true my friend, my head-dancer,
that at night when dreamers are asleep
and the moon alights on the huddling hills,
the stopped-up tombs are emptied?
I summon my shade: I am waiting
Come to me, come once more.

Appear to me just as you were
when I last saw you
sickly-pale as river mud
dragged still bloodstained to the pyre.
Or come to me like faint starlight
the thinnest birdcall, airy wraith—
or even as a horrid vision,
I don't much care.

I call you back
not to speak to you of war
or to reproach us both.
I don't want to know what the shades know
or even to tell you I repented
publicly of you. I am missing you.
I love you still. Know this:
I am still yours.

There, under the stone walls of his city
Bronze nibs tattooed him
With his own graveside speech

And his little soul fled nimbly into the hills

But a heavy curtain has fallen
Over this empty stage
The report was brought by an indifferent witness
And indifferently I turned my face
How I once burned and trembled at his name
Leant at my window
Weak with love—until he came
Touched me with his calloused fingers

Where did it all go? Poor credulous shade

Those memories—
I feel nothing for them

My debt is paid.

IX. THIRD DREAM

HELEN is in a room alone. PARIS has gone.

I was in a tour coach. It smelt of diesel and we were driving along winding roads on the outskirts of a city, towards the stadium, the TV tower and the crematoria.

We passed a double-headed signpost indicating the city limits, and about then our tour guide pointed out a massive fortress on a rocky promontory—I think we were heading that way. But first we were to visit an armed forces superstore. It was the biggest of its kind anywhere. Here the soldiers bought their uniforms, their cuirasses and helmets, pikes and staffs. But here too you could buy souvenirs (or so our guide told us) metal badges and sets of knucklebones. Little discs you could engrave with a gnomic line or two, a plea to the gods. That sort of thing.

The shop was large and well-appointed, surprisingly modern with turnstiles at the entry. But to enter you had to strip down: the young recruits baring their bottoms like children on an Edwardian postcard. I stood outside, looking in...

X. THE MESSENGER'S DESCENT

In every block in every room
The light grew dimmer, the air danker
The same oilcloth glimmered beneath a common moon.

Hermes slept under a coat, puttees wrapped round his ankles.
When he woke to use the lav the chain shone with hoar.

Outside the rank grass was glazed
The black trees bare. He stumbled
In his unlaced boots and swore
Clutching the knot at his waist.

In the underworld women lit spills of paper
And dropped them to flare in the stairwells
So those that followed would not lose their step,
But up here there was no way to find his darling
In the darkness and the loneliness.

He fumbled for the remote control and lay on his belly
Shivering, illuminated the box, the cold glare of the telly
Writhing with shapes he couldn't at first tease apart
(Hardly human shapes, without the usual fleshy hue)
Tinged with a heatless raddle, bleached in reckitt's blue.

Imagine you carried a vast boulder in a flimsy cart
Brought up from the mines in a wasted place
Drawing it a thousand miles through forests, over fast waters
Till you reached the yard where customs men were quartered
On the eve of war.

And even though they raced
To prepare their arms, to sandbag the barracks,
Still they stopped to stare at your unblinking freight
And came with hammer and wedges to investigate
How skilfully they mined the rock along unseen cracks
Sending shivers and faults into its uncloven skull
So at last it parted itself with a sort of moan
(One that might have stirred a heart of stone)
And the rock's hemispheres, as if released from a spell
Toppled, rocked and were still, surrounded by astounded men:
Two deep pools, jagged with crystals, swirling blood
And silver moons, enamel green, speckled with a flood
Of gold stars; a panner's dream, a dragon's den
Of stolen treasures sparkling in a midden
And here and there shot through with opalescence—
Minerals destined to be carved into eggs. But imperial
    obsolescence
And war intervened.
                    So the rock was hidden
In the safe room of a provincial customs yard
And you were told to disappear, save your hide
Because a war was coming.
                        Then you too died
And there was no one left to remember the glittering hoard.

At the end of a broken road, lost without trace
The spectrum blazed, the stone's livid seams
Flickered with infinite small stone-dreams
And something like a smile slid over its face—

So feathered Hermes, wrapped in blankets on a cot
Sat up agape to see the brilliance of that screen:
Golden figures in fur and masks of lambent green,
An iridescent rainbow descending to its golden pot

And over every image a pair of livid lips
Seemed to speak to him
In the silent voice of an uneasy dream
Incessantly opening and pressing together in hypnotic loops.

At length he ran his palm across his brow
And stood to find his way back to the stove

A crust of ice clanked in the kettle—
The matches only fizzed
Guttering in his cupped hand.

This part is painful to repeat.
                             It frightens me
To lay such details out in print.
I want to let it wander off the page
Or, like lamplight on marble, fade
To the milky facet of a flint

But it can only be as it is.

In the dark room the colours gathered themselves
Convulsed, swam forth and filled the room
Were changed:

Purple and vermilion bruises, darker lesions,
Yellow barred with angry scars
The shape a toecap leaves on a shin
The ghastly tone of once-inhabited skin.

  I bent over retching and my head was a vessel
  Of dark fluid under a film of grease
  No light no sky as when a tiny boat
  Disappears into a vale of stormy seas

There will be some who say that this must be
For what full-born vision can be conjured
Into life without gibbet and dungeon.
But, let it be known, it was not me.

Narrative appals me
Narrative plus rhyme is like
A schoolteacher in an abandoned city
Crouched in her pulpit
Tugging at her ripped skirt

A woman dreams of her wedding
And wakes to find tattered muslin
Fluttering at an open hole

A couple plan their nuptials
Wandering the aisles of a wedding fair
But on the happy day
The wedding palace vanishes

Into burning air

Go as far as you please
travel any path
but the plummet sounds only depth.

Remember sitting in the bath as a child
and watching a tiny sailboat on the surface
and knowing suddenly the vast leagues
of water under its keel

Remember sticking your head sideways into a doll's house
gluing yourself to a peephole
lying next to a doll, squinting,
the doll a round pink hill rising above you

Or holding a plane high over your head
a bomber with all its tiny eggs slung underneath
and dashing it down on the tiles.

How your stylite soul stood tall
above your small self
How proportion swung like a magic door,
once so small, and now your height
in the labyrinth wall.

So Gods in the bronze attic
throw themselves into mortal poses
around a piece of tired baize
where countless heroes are arranged.

You can see them if you know where to look:
like the tiny creator in the fisheye mirror
behind the childlike couple
They sign their names on every wall

They gaze through the window
willing their magic eyes to shrink
their own bodies.

Gods ask themselves:

- What are favourite games with dolls—washing, feeding,
  making clothes, dressing and undressing, brushing hair,
  putting to sleep, talking to, punishing, &c.?

- How are dolls treated? What discipline, rewards,
  punishments? With what objects?

- Are dolls put to sleep? Is it important that they should
  be able to close their eyes? Any lullabies?

- Are there any magical uses to which dolls are put? Do
  they resemble magical images, idols, &c.?

For the length of their game
they desire to enter the miniature hearts of mortals
to play from within.

It's an ordinary day late in the year
And in the flicker of an eye the world
Is revealed to be a tent on a battlefield

Stones sing on the river bank
The desert stretches itself and pants
The umbrella pines are presentiments

gods weave around each other
barely touching
sniffing one another's genitalia
saying nothing

for gods all things are fair and just
even a fly on the eye of the royal armourer—
whereas mortals are split between care and lust
following the path of the directionless cockchafer

There was once an egg
the biggest egg in the world
and it grew and grew until it was so
so big it couldn't be moved from the eye where it lay
the largest eye in the world
set deep in the deepest socket
deeper than the hull of the Titanic
deeper than the sea itself. . .
— *like, this deep!* (says the god) *space-deep*
(dancing and spreading his arms as wide as wings)
— *very   very   deep*
(opening his own eyes so wide they float above his head)
But imagine now
all that depth concertinaed up
a million little folds, a million billion creases
folded and folded and folded until it's. . .
— *tiny weeny*
weeny teeny

— *stuffed into a little capsule, a . . . a what . . .*
a locket?
— *yes!*
and the locket put in a jewellery box? And the jewellery box
into a hidden drawer?
— *yes, a secret one! One only a king would know about!*
and the secret drawer inside another drawer . . .
— *and that drawer in a campaign chest.*
and that campaign chest in a tent . . .
— *and the tent stands on a plain.*
a wide plain . . .
— *This plain is covered in tiny tents, so very many of them.*
but this one is of elaborate gold-painted canvas.
— *In it a hero walks up and down.*
yes, he walks up and down in anguish and rage
(pause)
— *but he is not the subject of this story?*
no
(hesitates)
not him.

> *gods are curled in sleeping positions*
> *but their eyes still gleam*
> *only mortals turn away from the world*
> *into the privacy of dream*

XII. FOURTH DREAM

HELEN *is lying on a straw pallet.*

I took everyone to the station, saw them onto their trains. In other dreams I have taken trains myself on long journeys, on railway lines that passed beyond borders into trackless lands, through tundra, wild places.

All these dreams of travel were present in this dream, they were dream memories inside it—I could have opened them up like celestial table cloths and spread them out as their own dreams... But I didn't. This time I was sending off others instead.

When the trains had rolled out and away I returned alone to the walled yard. And when the man with the scarifying knife said it was my turn I lay down on the ground. It didn't hurt but it was shameful, and an old woman said it should never have happened.

I should tell someone. But who can I tell? My wounds are not painful—but small nodes like buds have begun to appear in them.

XIII. THE LIMPET GATHERER

Many years before
Trojan elders built a semaphore system
Stretching from the city across the plain
So help could be summoned from the sea.

The Gods helped stick towers in place on the sands.
Such tiny moving parts! Arms that lift! Flags that cock!
And language in code. The Gods adore a coded language.
They often send encrypted messages
But forget to send the key.

The towers were elaborate, with pulleys and lines
Bronze paddles flashing prettily.
It was a wondrous sight on the plain.
But when the Gods saw the mortals
Busily operating this line of glinting towers
They changed their minds
And declared a war.

The towers stood motionless.
The ropes rotted. The flags faded.
Time passed and no one remembered
Why they even stood there.
It was thought that gods had built them.
In a way this was true.

But Slip-a-knife the limpet gatherer
Still slept in a hut at the foot of a tower

At the river's mouth
Waking each day to polish the hands of the machine.

He rose at dawn and squatted on the riverbank.
Sometimes the water was sluggish
Sometimes, like today, it gushed down to the sea
Splitting on snags and showing its jade corners.
He felt kingfishers zip by, sudden threads of blue neon—
He heard creatures stirring in the banks
Saw a shadow of something swimming upstream
Flit between the reeds.

Slip-a-knife fetched his oilskin bundle as he did every morning
And opened it out on the stone threshold.
Here were his precious objects:
First, his broad little knife for limpets.
Three multi-coloured glass beads with eyes on.
A rusty buckle frame. A sparrowhawk feather.
A metal mirror from a telescope. A toothless comb.
Some twine carefully folded. He smiled to see the last:
A coin with a labyrinth etched on it, found in the river
Washed up by an eddy tide. He rubbed it with spit
Wiped it on his polishing cloth. He knew that story alright!

Slip-a-knife take care! Slip-a-knife hide your jewels!
There are eyes in the reeds watching you!
Maybe toads, maybe not.
Maybe fat carp blinking
Or maybe not.

Slip-a-knife returned the bundle to its hiding place.
He began his polishing. He polished all day in the hot sun
And the light flashed off the bronze paddles

Like small bright planets hovering over the plain
Flash! Flash! Slip-a-knife, take care!

Slip-a-knife never saw his assassin
Never knew if it was god or man that prized him
From the rock
Inserting the stumpy blade of fate and twisting.
So poor Slip-a-knife was loosened from life forever.

When Odysseus gives blood to the seer
Slip-a-knife standing close feels the touch
Of a drop of blood on his unsheathed soul
And speaks to Odysseus:

> never mind my unburied body my bog-ballast self
> but return to the plain friend and retrieve my wealth
> put it into my leathery arms where I rest
> give me my baubles—they are all I possess.

Odysseus is disgusted with such common materialism.
He shuns the limpet-gatherer's ghost—

Slip-a-knife's hoard remains lost.

XIV. THE TICKET BOOTH

Papa War
Father War
King War

When we brought you to the crematorium
the lid slid off your cardboard coffin in the heat.

The bus jangled along the road and a scrap of your sleeve
was visible—
not your head, thank god
not your shrunken head.

You lay on the ground between us,
all our black-stockinged calves,
and one of your raving daughters straightened the lid
as if it were nothing untoward.

It was hot in the bus, it smelt of mazut
and a faintly disagreeable scent—yours, Daddy.
One of your bald wives
sprayed the air with perfume.

If I close my eyes we could be on a gently rocking boat
taking you out to deep waters
your pockets filled with black stones
your little eyes covered with two coins.

Heads or tails, Father? Do we dare change course?
It was said you made men slaves or made them free

but here we are, your daughters
your wives, dressed in mourning weeds.

You, Papa, died a vassal
in a basement of groaning men.
I shall never forget you, Papochka
till it happens again.

I lit a match. The room was full of sleeping bodies.
I had already walked among them and touched them
   with my feet
But you've heard it said that love and regal dignity are
   rarely found together.

   we must wrap these men in shrouds, I said,
   for everything I see is death
   and everything I touch is dead
   and all that was safely moored is now untethered

But the words came out hoarse and incomprehensible
As if a brute steer lowed in my throat
And I was ushered on
With a tug on the rope,
Given to understand that my own quarters
Lay somewhere beyond.

Now I carried another on my back,
The lightest presence
It lay its head against my neck.

I had been billeted to a ticket booth:
Eight glass windows looked out on a dark strand.

Perhaps a ferry stopped here once
Its last halt before turning away from land.

My passenger slipped to the ground
Took a crown of flowers from her head
And placed it on mine.

She stroked my dewlap as if it were a harp
And I stood, virginal, vast
Uneasily stirring my silken flanks
While my little king disported herself.

    alas she disappeared
    my king, my liege

    like breath in cold air
    she rose and was dispersed

    pretty child
    and I
    disconsolate
    cursed
    wild

    a steer on a rope

    found no words
    and little hope

But from my booth, in eight frames
I saw the whole proceedings:

I saw a fleet of boats heave up against the sky

I saw us emerging from the flaming trees

I saw our animal heads melt in fiery birth

I saw a priest come forward to bless a tank

I saw a direct hit on a philosopher's hearth

I saw the lonely tiger's massive eye

I saw a shoebill crouching in a sink

I saw a dystrophic man lift up a lyre